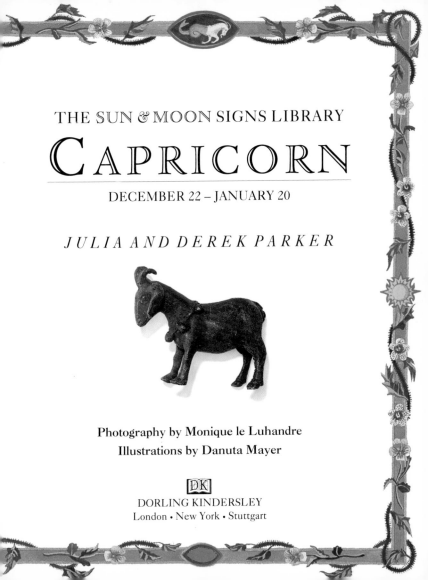

THE SUN & MOON SIGNS LIBRARY

CAPRICORN

DECEMBER 22 – JANUARY 20

JULIA AND DEREK PARKER

Photography by Monique le Luhandre
Illustrations by Danuta Mayer

DK

DORLING KINDERSLEY
London · New York · Stuttgart

Dedicated to Jan Leeming

DK

A DORLING KINDERSLEY BOOK

Editor **Tom Fraser**
Art Editor **Ursula Dawson**
Managing Editor **Krystyna Mayer**
Managing Art Editor **Derek Coombes**
Production **Antony Heller**
U.S. Editor **Laaren Brown**

Computer page make-up Patrizio Semproni.
Photography p 10 © Michael Holford/British Museum; p 11 CM Dixon/
British Museum; p 16 Tim Ridley. Stylist pp 28-29 Lucy Elworthy.
Illustration pp 60-61 Kuo Kang Chen. Jacket illustration Peter Lawman.
With thanks to Carolyn Lancaster and John Filbey.

First American Edition, 1992
10 9 8 7 6 5 4 3 2 1

Published in the United States by
Dorling Kindersley, Inc., 232 Madison Avenue
New York, N.Y. 10016

Library of Congress Catalog Card Number 92-52793
ISBN 1-56458-093-8

Reproduced by GRB Editrice, Verona, Italy
Printed and bound in Hong Kong by Imago

CONTENTS

INTRODUCING
CAPRICORN

CAPRICORN, WHO IS TRADITIONALLY REPRESENTED AS THE
HALF-GOAT, HALF-FISH FIGURE, IS THE TENTH SIGN OF
THE ZODIAC. SUN SIGN CAPRICORNIANS GENERALLY HAVE
RATHER COMPLEX CHARACTERS.

There are two distinct types of
Capricornian. One type will be
ambitious and enterprising, while the
other will never find the motivation to
move forward in life and will spend a
great deal of time complaining about
the real or imagined obstacles that
hold them back. Even the most
famous and successful Capricornian
may have a tendency to grumble, and
all people of this sign can feel that
they are forced to carry undeserved
burdens. A fondness for solitude is
another Capricornian characteristic.

Traditional groupings
As you read through this book you
will come across references to the
elements and the qualities, and to
positive and negative, or masculine
and feminine signs.

The first of these groupings, that of
the elements, comprises fire, earth,
air, and water signs. The second, that
of the qualities, divides the Zodiac

into cardinal, fixed, and mutable
signs. The final grouping is made up
of positive and negative, or masculine
and feminine signs. Each Zodiac sign
is associated with a combination of
components from these groupings, all
of which contribute different
characteristics to it.

Capricornian characteristics
Capricorn belongs to the earth
element, and its subjects often have a
great deal of practical common sense.
It is of the cardinal quality, which may
make you outgoing. However, as a
negative, feminine sign Capricorn also
inclines its subjects to introversion.
All of these characteristics find
expression in the Capricorn
personality. Saturn, your ruling planet,
also guides your destiny, and
"saturnine" is an adjective that often
applies to you. Capricornians
generally prefer subdued colors such
as gray or dark green.

ARIES
PISCES
AQUARIUS
CAPRICORN
SAGITTARIUS
SCORPIO
LIBRA
VIRGO
LEO
CANCER
GEMINI
TAURUS

The Zodiac Wheel

The relationship between each Zodiac sign and the traditional astrological groupings is made clear within the Zodiac wheel. As you read through this book you will also discover references to polar, or opposite signs, and these, too, can be easily worked out by referring to the wheel.

FIRE

CARDINAL   EARTH

MASCULINE   MUTABLE   AIR

FEMININE   FIXED   WATER

MYTHS & LEGENDS

THE ZODIAC, WHICH IS BELIEVED TO HAVE ORIGINATED IN
BABYLON AS LONG AS 2,500 YEARS AGO, IS A
CIRCLE OF CONSTELLATIONS THROUGH WHICH THE SUN
MOVES DURING THE COURSE OF A YEAR.

Many Zodiacal figures were first carved on Babylonian boundary stones. This is where Capricorn makes his first appearance, as the Goat-Fish. He is shown as Ea, a man walking in a great fish-shaped cloak, with the fish head over his head and the cloak trailing into a tail. One of his Babylonian titles was "antelope of the subterranean ocean." He was said to rise from the waters during the day in order to tutor man in the arts of civilization and to return to the depths at night.

Ea's name means "House of the Water," and perhaps this indicates the significance that was placed upon him in a country where water was such a precious commodity. He had the role

Pan pipes
*This bronze statuette of
Pan and the syrinx dates
from 430 B.C.*

of god of knowledge and presided over the work done by men. Because of this, he was devoutly worshiped by many different types of craftsmen.

Later myths

The later mythological associations of Capricorn are obscure and difficult to follow. There is a distant association with Pan, no doubt because although he had a human torso and arms, other parts of his body consisted of the legs, ears, and horns of a goat. He was the son of Hermes, the messenger of the gods, but his mother's name is uncertain. According to some sources it was Callisto, but others sometimes mention Penelope.

Pan and Syrinx

Pan is perhaps best remembered as the being who was responsible for inventing the panpipes; he called them syrinx in honor of a nymph who was turned into a reed to escape his amorous attentions.

Pan loved mountains, caves, and lonely places, and it was while frisking with nymphs in one such desolate place that he gave chase to Syrinx. Just as he was about to capture her, she called out for help to her father, Ladon the river god. At her request, Ladon turned her into a reed and Pan was foiled. To console himself, Pan cut down a clump of reeds and made some pipes. The music that Pan was able to produce on his syrinx was apparently so sweet that on one occasion he challenged Apollo, the god of music and the personification of beauty, to a musical competition.

Panic fear

The feeling of loneliness that can afflict people traveling on their own through wild or inhospitable terrain was sometimes attributed to the presence of Pan. Any fear that seemed unattributable to an obvious cause has come to be known as "panic fear" – or panic for short.

The music of Pan
The image on this dish, which dates from 1515, shows Pan playing his syrinx to a couple of shepherds.

Although it does at first seem to be an extremely slender association, astrologers throughout the ages have attempted to play up with the Capricornian qualities that can be related to the goat.

The domestic animal is, for instance, often tethered in one small space, while for the wild mountain goat the mountains and hills seem to be as accessible as they once were to the god Pan himself.

Many Sun sign Capricornians have a fondness and perhaps even a real need for solitude.

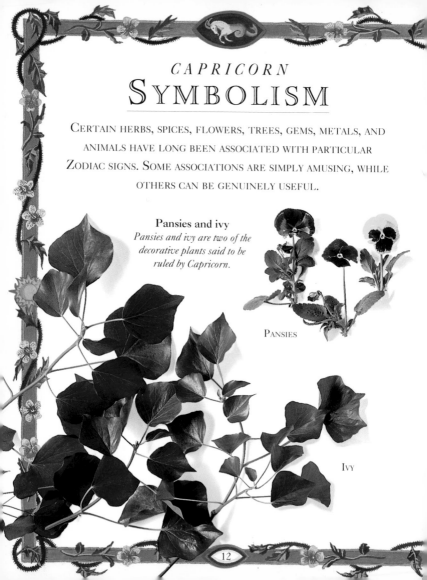

CAPRICORN
SYMBOLISM

CERTAIN HERBS, SPICES, FLOWERS, TREES, GEMS, METALS, AND
ANIMALS HAVE LONG BEEN ASSOCIATED WITH PARTICULAR
ZODIAC SIGNS. SOME ASSOCIATIONS ARE SIMPLY AMUSING, WHILE
OTHERS CAN BE GENUINELY USEFUL.

Pansies and ivy
*Pansies and ivy are two of the
decorative plants said to be
ruled by Capricorn.*

PANSIES

IVY

Spices
No spice is traditionally associated with Capricorn, but angostura bitters and cloves are sometimes attributed to this sign.

CLOVES

BELLADONNA

Trees
Capricornian trees include the somewhat austere pine and yew, as well as the graceful willow, aspen, elm, and poplar.

Herbs
The poisonous belladonna is ruled by Capricorn. Knapweed, which is good for healing sores, and plantain, which is used almost indiscriminately to treat a wide variety of illnesses, are also traditional Capricornian herbs.

KNAPWEED

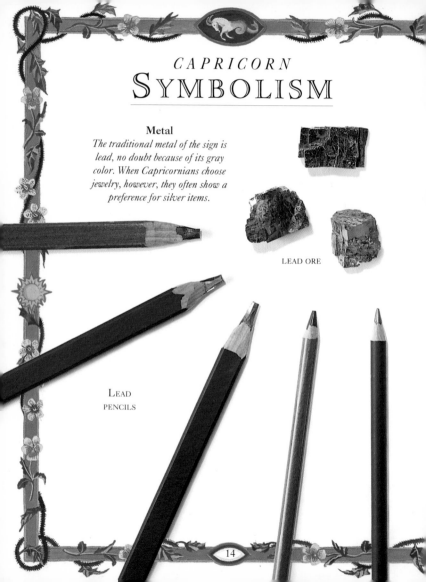

CAPRICORN

SYMBOLISM

Metal

The traditional metal of the sign is lead, no doubt because of its gray color. When Capricornians choose jewelry, however, they often show a preference for silver items.

LEAD ORE

LEAD
PENCILS

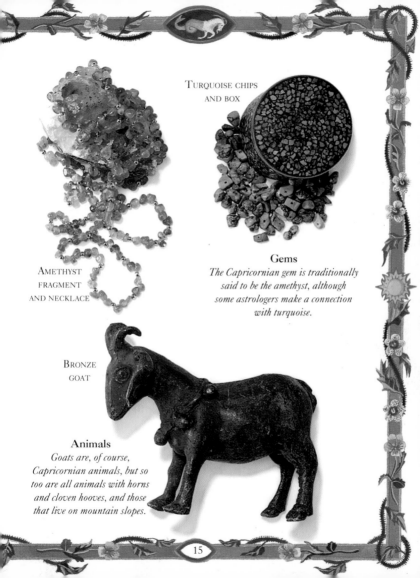

TURQUOISE CHIPS
AND BOX

AMETHYST
FRAGMENT
AND NECKLACE

Gems
The Capricornian gem is traditionally said to be the amethyst, although some astrologers make a connection with turquoise.

BRONZE
GOAT

Animals
Goats are, of course, Capricornian animals, but so too are all animals with horns and cloven hooves, and those that live on mountain slopes.

CAPRICORN
PROFILE

YOUR OVERALL LOOK WILL BE CONVENTIONAL WITHIN YOUR OWN
PEER GROUP. CAPRICORNIANS USUALLY WALK QUICKLY,
TAKING LONG STRIDES. THEY HOLD THEIR HEADS EITHER UP OR
DOWN, ACCORDING TO THEIR PREVAILING MOOD.

Many Capricornians are tall, and they may have a tendency to stoop, sometimes with their knees bent. However, when they are feeling positive they will stand erect and tall, and may occasionally appear to look down on the rest of the world.

The Capricornian face
A high forehead and a direct gaze characterize the Capricorn face.

The body

As Capricorn rules the bones, the skeletal frame is likely to be strong, with rather obvious bony wrists, elbows, and knees. A large number of Capricornians are tall and thin, with a fairly gaunt appearance. Another type of Capricornian will have a slim build, but will often be on the short side. Members of this second group can tend to have rather bony knees.

Capricornian legs are likely to be long and slim and, in the case of many women, extremely beautiful. They will quite rightly be shown to their best advantage, for example, swathed in black hosiery.

The face

Capricornians often have rather heavy hair, which tends to be sleekly styled and cut. The forehead can be high, and the eyes show directness; they are steady, although perhaps downcast. The nose is often emphasized by lines joining its sides to the corners of the mouth, which are usually turned down when the individual smiles. The chin can sometimes be fairly sharp. The shape of the entire face – the temples,

The Capricornian stance
Capricornians are often tall, perhaps with a tendency to stoop. When feeling positive they will, however, stand tall and proud.

nose, cheekbones, jaw, and chin – may reflect the rather prominent Capricornian bone structure.

Style

The Capricornian image is conventional: both men and women look marvelous in well-cut, chic suits and dark colors. A "little black dress," perhaps adorned by dramatic jewelry, is a particular favorite with women. Stylishness is the rule, even with casual clothes. Quality is important, too, and you are likely to favor designer labels. Exaggerated fashion will not appeal to you; classic clothes will.

In general

Capricornians do not like to stand out in a crowd. A reserved, quiet image is far more acceptable. Because you like to impress, but will be reluctant to make too strong a statement, you will often choose to wear high-quality, formal clothes. With experience, you will discover ways in which a dramatic but restrained look can be achieved by the addition of subtle and interesting jewelry or accessories. Capricornians tend to be attracted to high-quality belts, handbags, and briefcases. You may also have a preference for traditional fragrances, as opposed to more overpowering modern scents.

Clothes made from natural fibers such as cotton and wool, perhaps in shades of pale gray and dark green, are likely to flatter you.

CAPRICORN
PERSONALITY

CAPRICORNIANS SHOULD SET THEIR SIGHTS HIGH AND ASPIRE TO
GREAT THINGS. MANY ARE TRUE ACHIEVERS, BUT
OTHERS TEND TO GRUMBLE OVER THE OBSTACLES THAT
PREVENT THEM FROM BEING SUCCESSFUL.

Many fine and noble qualities, for example prudence, caution, circumspection, and practical common sense, are shared by members of this Sun sign group. However, unlike the other Zodiac signs, this one produces two very contrasting types.

The symbol of the sign is a goat with a fish's tail, and this fact is significant. The fish's tail represents a powerful psychological factor in the Capricornian makeup that can curb ambition, produce a negative response to other people's suggestions, and generally spoil things not only for the Capricornian, but for others as well.

At work
You may sometimes take on a gloomy attitude because you feel that much of your success at work depends on your being thoroughly reliable in what you do, so that you must stick to a regular routine. This could make you feel perennially depressed.

You will no doubt place great value upon retaining a sense of security, and are unlikely to take extravagant risks.

Your attitudes
Your depressing inner voice will all too often make itself felt when you try to be at all daring, or want to do something just for the fun of it. Try not to let it hold you back.

There is, however, another, fun-loving side to the Capricornian goat. Many people of this sign seem to manage metaphorically to slough off the fish's tail and become all goat – in fact, a giddy goat who simply will not have anything to do with the wet-blanket, depressive attitude expressed by some Capricornians. They will have fun, love life, and thoroughly enjoy the process of achieving the ambitious objectives that they decide to set themselves. These latter Capricornians are able to take care of themselves very well.

Saturn rules Capricorn
*Saturn, originally an agricultural god, represents the
Capricornian ruling planet. It can make its subjects practical
and cautious, but also selfish and narrow-minded.*

They are highly motivated people who will attempt to reach for the sky, and may well go so far as to touch it.

The overall picture

You should try to recognize which type of Capricorn you resemble most closely. Remember, however, that yours is one sign, not two; you may seem to be a placid valley goat, happily tethered to a restricting pole, but you can escape and play the giddy goat. You might lack confidence, but this should not be allowed to hold you back. Even the most successful person is, of course, entitled to grumble from time to time, but you should be aware of how this tendency affects you and those around you, and try not to succumb to it too often.

CAPRICORN
ASPIRATIONS

YOUR NEED FOR SECURITY CAN CONFLICT WITH AMBITION, AND
YOU MAY NOT LIKE TAKING CHANCES. A FONDNESS
FOR ROUTINE MAKES YOU A VALUABLE EMPLOYEE, AND YOU
MAY HAVE WHAT IT TAKES TO COPE WITH A TOP JOB.

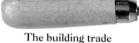

The building trade
In the same way that Capricornians are
excellent at "building" their lives, you
may find inner satisfaction from working
in the building trades.

TROWEL
AND
CEMENT

MINIATURE
GLOBE

Property management
Managing the land is an attractive
profession for Capricornians. You
will enjoy working on site as
much as in an office.

Teaching
The dry Capricornian
sense of humor will be an
asset to you if you decide to
become a teacher. You
may specialize in
geography.

20

DOCUMENTS AND WAX SEAL

Civil service
A need for security and the chance to make gradual progress, plus the possibility of involvement with those in power, attracts Capricornians to civil service.

APPLICATOR FOR
DENTAL CEMENT

PLANS AND
SPIRIT LEVEL

Dentistry
The powerful astrological tradition linking Capricorn with the skeletal system could draw you to the dental profession.

CAPRICORN
HEALTH

CAPRICORNIANS ARE OFTEN TOO CONCERNED WITH WORLDLY
MATTERS AND CARRY HEAVY BURDENS OF RESPONSIBILITY;
YOU MAY TEND TO NEGLECT YOUR PHYSICAL WELL-BEING AND
COULD AGE MORE QUICKLY THAN YOU SHOULD.

The Capricornian body area covers the knees and shins, but the skin, bones, and teeth are also ruled by this sign. It is important for all Sun sign Capricornians, both young and old, to keep moving. An excessively static life may result in stiffness of the joints, and rheumatism and even arthritis could set in.

Your diet

Most Capricornians have a rather fast metabolism, so weight gain is less likely to be a problem for you than other Zodiac types. You might benefit from adding the cell salt calcium phosphate (calc. phos.) to your diet. As the principal salt contained in the bone structure, it may be of particular importance to you.

Taking care

Many Capricornians are interested in sports, and some may be great athletes. You could find that knee injuries will affect you more frequently than they do people of other signs. Make sure that you get medical attention for even the slightest trouble; more severe problems may develop if you are at all negligent in this area.

Even if regular dental checkups appear to be little more than an unnecessary expense, they are especially desirable for Capricornians. You might feel justifiably proud when the dentist congratulates you on your high level of oral hygiene, but you should not take this as an excuse to stop making regular visits.

As a Capricornian you may well possess unusually beautiful, fine skin, and that too could need some extra-special care. It may be ultrasensitive, in which case it would be advisable for you to use a high-factor protective cream in very strong sun to prevent redness, blotchiness, or something more serious from developing.

Astrology and the body

For many centuries it was not possible to practice medicine without a knowledge of astrology. In European universities, medical training included information on how planetary positions would affect the administration of medicines, the bleeding of patients, and the right time to pick herbs and make potions. Each Zodiac sign rules a particular part of the body – from Aries (the head) to Pisces (the feet) – and textbooks always included a drawing of a "Zodiac man" (or woman) that illustrated the point.

CAPRICORN AT
LEISURE

EACH OF THE SUN SIGNS TRADITIONALLY SUGGESTS SPARE-TIME
ACTIVITIES, HOBBIES, AND VACATION SPOTS.
ALTHOUGH THESE ARE ONLY SUGGESTIONS, THEY OFTEN WORK
OUT WELL FOR CAPRICORNIANS.

Going to the races
*A day at the races involves
dressing up and mixing with the
"right" people, and therefore
gives satisfaction to
ambitious Capricornians.*

BINOCULARS

MODEL SPINNING
WHEEL

Weaving
*The creation of fabrics
from natural materials may
prove attractive to creative
Capricornians.*

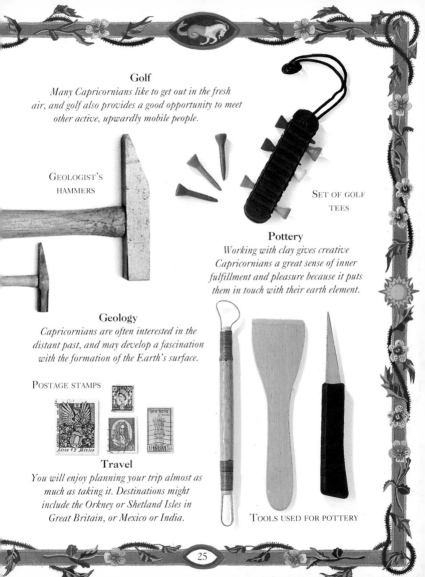

Golf
Many Capricornians like to get out in the fresh air, and golf also provides a good opportunity to meet other active, upwardly mobile people.

GEOLOGIST'S
HAMMERS

SET OF GOLF
TEES

Pottery
Working with clay gives creative Capricornians a great sense of inner fulfillment and pleasure because it puts them in touch with their earth element.

Geology
Capricornians are often interested in the distant past, and may develop a fascination with the formation of the Earth's surface.

POSTAGE STAMPS

Travel
You will enjoy planning your trip almost as much as taking it. Destinations might include the Orkney or Shetland Isles in Great Britain, or Mexico or India.

TOOLS USED FOR POTTERY

CAPRICORN IN
LOVE

CAPRICORNIANS USUALLY KEEP THEIR EMOTIONS UNDER CONTROL
AND CAN BE PEOPLE OF FEW WORDS. WHAT THEY DO SAY,
HOWEVER, THEY USUALLY MEAN. TO ACHIEVE FULFILLING LOVE
LIVES, THEY SOMETIMES NEED TO LEARN HOW TO RELAX.

Very possibly, it may take some time for you to realize you are in love. Once you fall for someone, however, your commitment will be deep. Your natural caution encourages you to make quite sure of your ground before committing yourself, or even before declaring your love. You may fear the thought of rejection, and it is likely to hurt you much more than it would most other Zodiac types.

As a lover

You can be very reserved indeed in the way that you express your feelings towards others, and may even take this to the point where you give the distinct impression of being rather cold and distant. This characteristic is most likely to emerge if you had a repressive or overly disciplined childhood. But with the right partner, all Capricornians will blossom and show their fun-loving characteristics. Your tendency always to do the right and proper thing will help to ensure your fidelity once you are committed to a permanent relationship. When this occurs, a strong urge to protect and look after your partner and, in due course, your children, will probably develop in you. If, however, you are

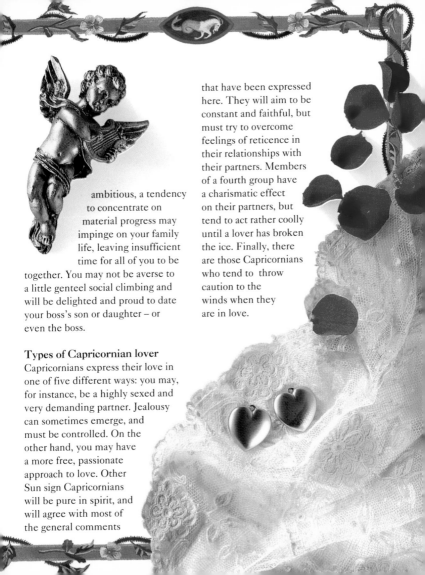

ambitious, a tendency to concentrate on material progress may impinge on your family life, leaving insufficient time for all of you to be together. You may not be averse to a little genteel social climbing and will be delighted and proud to date your boss's son or daughter – or even the boss.

Types of Capricornian lover
Capricornians express their love in one of five different ways: you may, for instance, be a highly sexed and very demanding partner. Jealousy can sometimes emerge, and must be controlled. On the other hand, you may have a more free, passionate approach to love. Other Sun sign Capricornians will be pure in spirit, and will agree with most of the general comments that have been expressed here. They will aim to be constant and faithful, but must try to overcome feelings of reticence in their relationships with their partners. Members of a fourth group have a charismatic effect on their partners, but tend to act rather coolly until a lover has broken the ice. Finally, there are those Capricornians who tend to throw caution to the winds when they are in love.

CAPRICORN AT
HOME

DEPENDING ON WHAT TYPE OF CAPRICORNIAN YOU ARE, YOUR
HOME WILL EITHER BE FURNISHED AND DESIGNED CHIEFLY
TO IMPRESS OR EXTREMELY SPARTAN. YOU WILL PROCLAIM YOUR
TRUE PERSONALITY THROUGH THE STYLE YOU CHOOSE.

Many Capricornians move from one residence to the next with unusual frequency. This is generally due to the fact that as they gradually make their way up the social ladder they want their homes to match their newfound status accordingly.

China coffee set

Articles made from china or fine porcelain are likely to be proudly displayed.

Furniture

Financially conscious Capricornians are highly unlikely to throw money away on trendy or impractical flippancies. This holds particularly true when it comes to their choice of furniture.

Your taste is possibly rather conventional, so you will choose traditional styles and, if you can afford them, antiques that are made in a traditional fashion. To obtain them you will often search at auction

houses rather than large department stores. You are probably attracted to beautiful, good-quality, wood, either polished or left in its natural state. One thing that might well be worth bearing in mind is the Capricornian tendency to want to impress other people. This could end up governing your choice and, as a result, comfort may be sacrificed in a search for the correct type of appearance.

Soft furnishings

You will usually keep soft furnishings to a minimum. Curtains and drapes will be well shaped and cut, and perhaps made of natural materials such as linen. Pure silk may be another favorite with you. Your

preference for natural materials is due to the influence of the earth element of your sign. The overall effect of the Capricornian home is elegant, tasteful, and without doubt expensive-looking, even if the individual is poor. A certain severity can, however, also be present.

Decorative objects

Any inherited articles will be proudly displayed, especially if they are silver, and family portraits will be placed in prominent positions.

A tendency to show off objects on stands is common. Capricornians are often attracted to unusual rocks or shells. You may have a piece of amethyst, the Capricornian stone, glinting away on a windowsill. A restrained flower arrangement containing a few carefully placed blooms may also have a place in your home. China or pieces of porcelain will often be carefully displayed.

Gingham cloth
Materials with a subdued pattern often characterize the Capricornian home.

Elegant armchair
Settees and easy chairs may be covered in natural materials, such as wool, and are likely to be rather hard.

THE
MOON
AND
YOU

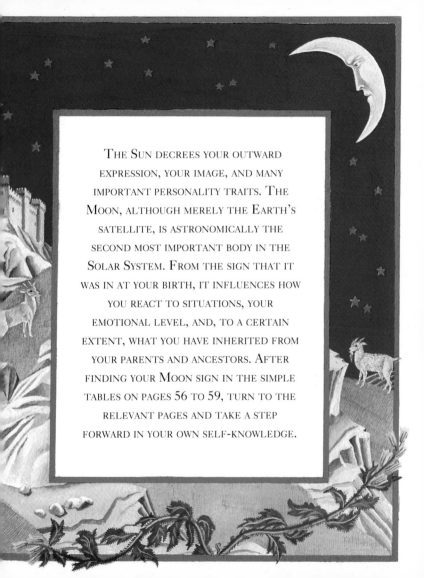

THE SUN DECREES YOUR OUTWARD
EXPRESSION, YOUR IMAGE, AND MANY
IMPORTANT PERSONALITY TRAITS. THE
MOON, ALTHOUGH MERELY THE EARTH'S
SATELLITE, IS ASTRONOMICALLY THE
SECOND MOST IMPORTANT BODY IN THE
SOLAR SYSTEM. FROM THE SIGN THAT IT
WAS IN AT YOUR BIRTH, IT INFLUENCES HOW
YOU REACT TO SITUATIONS, YOUR
EMOTIONAL LEVEL, AND, TO A CERTAIN
EXTENT, WHAT YOU HAVE INHERITED FROM
YOUR PARENTS AND ANCESTORS. AFTER
FINDING YOUR MOON SIGN IN THE SIMPLE
TABLES ON PAGES 56 TO 59, TURN TO THE
RELEVANT PAGES AND TAKE A STEP
FORWARD IN YOUR OWN SELF-KNOWLEDGE.

THE MOON IN
ARIES

YOUR ASSERTIVE ARIEN MOON PROVIDES YOU WITH A POSITIVE AND
ENTHUSIASTIC RESPONSE TO AMBITIOUS CAPRICORNIAN
OBJECTIVES AND SCHEMES. IT HELPS QUELL ANY TENDENCY
TO TAKE YOURSELF AND LIFE TOO SERIOUSLY.

You respond to most situations with a positive, lively enthusiasm that adds a sparkle to your practical, earthy Capricornian qualities. Your powerful motivation to be aspiring and ambitious is supported by an instinctive urge to win.

Self-expression
You have the potential to be a truly high achiever. Very few situations frighten you, and you are in an excellent position to overcome any inhibiting feelings. The emotional energy of your Arien Moon is very potent. Express it by getting involved in work that you find really rewarding.

Romance
You are among the most passionate of Capricornians, and may fall in love more quickly, and express yourself less cautiously, than many people of your Sun sign. Your partners will appreciate your positive approach to

this sphere of your life. Allow your passion plenty of free expression, and do not hesitate to sweep your lovers off their feet. The worst Arien fault is selfishness, and you should be aware that it may lead to problems.

Your well-being
The Arien body area is the head, and you may consequently be rather prone to headaches. These are probably stress-related, so perhaps you would benefit from a relaxation technique such as yoga. Otherwise, there is a relationship between headaches and the kidneys, and it is possible that yours could be slightly out of balance.

Ariens are hasty and prone to minor accidents. As a Sun sign Capricornian you have enough caution and patience to overcome this tendency, but you could sometimes become uncharacteristically careless. You usually cope very well with quite vigorous sports and exercise.

The Moon in Aries

Planning ahead

In true Capricornian style, you are probably careful with money and smart with investments. Your Arien Moon gives you an enterprising spirit that encourages you to start money-making schemes.

People with an Arien emphasis commonly have two sources of income; you may well fall successfully into this category. You are probably more generous than many Sun sign Capricornians, and your immediate response to any form of need is to take direct action, often by donating some money.

Parenthood

All Capricornians like to have some time to themselves, perhaps for reading or listening to music. Make sure that you have enough of this spare time. You should not find it difficult to keep up with your children's ideas, so the generation gap will pose few problems for you.

THE MOON IN
TAURUS

YOUR SUN AND MOON ARE BOTH IN EARTH SIGNS. YOUR TAUREAN
MOON COMPLEMENTS YOUR CAPRICORNIAN SUN, AND ADDS A
WARM AND AFFECTIONATE RESPONSE TO THE HIGHLY PRACTICAL,
MORE CAUTIOUS ASPECTS OF YOUR CHARACTER.

You are among the most practical and cautious of all Sun and Moon sign combinations. Your gift is for the steady, sound development of your talents and abilities, and for solid material growth.

Self-expression

It is worth remembering that there is a lively, almost flighty side to Capricorn. If, however, you are too concerned with your career and family, and with finding a way to ensure that your children have everything they need, your livelier qualities could be somewhat subdued.

The Moon is traditionally "well placed" in Taurus. This means that its influence on you is rather stronger than on many people. Among other traits, it emphasizes an attraction to the good life and pleasure-seeking. You should allow yourself to respond positively to this, since it will let you enjoy the fruits of your labors.

Romance

Your Taurean Moon encourages your instinctive need for emotional and material security. You need a stable, permanent relationship and a reliable partner with whom you can stride forward through life.

You are a warm and sensual lover, and should enjoy a rich and rewarding love and sex life. Do, however, remember that possessiveness is the worst Taurean fault, and that you could well be too overbearing toward a lover, perhaps creating a rather claustrophobic atmosphere.

Your well-being

The Taurean body area covers the neck and throat, and you should therefore take care of it.

Those with a Taurean emphasis are often somewhat lazy when it comes to exercise and can have a rather slow metabolism. This is not usually the case with Capricornians. If you are

The Moon in Taurus

prone to weight gain, you may need to make exercise a regular part of your no doubt well-planned life. You may also have quite a sweet tooth and a preference for rich foods. The calories, and the pounds, could have an effect on your figure.

Planning ahead
You have the capacity to be very good with money. You may even have chosen a career in banking or insurance. In any case, you will certainly make your money work for you. You will not want to take financial risks of any kind and will devote a great deal of care and thought to avoiding them.

Parenthood
While you are ambitious for your children and respond warmly to them, you may be very conventional and rather strict. Try hard to make a conscious effort to remain aware of their changing problems and concerns. Otherwise the generation gap is likely to yawn wide.

THE MOON IN
GEMINI

YOUR ASPIRING, AMBITIOUS QUALITIES ARE LIGHTENED BY YOUR
GEMINIAN MOON, WHICH MAKES YOU VERSATILE AND
SOMETIMES GIVES YOU A TENDENCY TO DITHER IN DAUNTING
SITUATIONS. YOU HAVE A GREAT SENSE OF HUMOR.

The earth element of your Capricornian Sun sign, and the air element of your Geminian Moon sign, suggest that you have many interesting facets to your personality.

Self-expression

You have a lighthearted, but intellectual, response to challenges, being both inquisitive and skeptical. You are extremely lively in debate and are happy to play devil's advocate just to get your point made.

You are less single-minded than most Capricornians, and a natural versatility, a disposition to do more than one thing at a time, makes you interesting company. You probably know a little about a great many things and may be the typical collector of useless trifles.

Being a good communicator, working in some branch of the media would probably be most fulfilling for you. If you manage to guard against

superficiality, you can certainly put the excellent qualities of your Geminian Moon to good use.

Romance

You may take your love life rather less seriously than many Capricornians, and can, at times, be quite flighty and flirtatious. You particularly enjoy the friendship stage of a new relationship, and friendship and intellectual rapport are essential in the long term. Your sex life may be both lively and experimental, and you should take this into account when forming a relationship. Bear in mind the Geminian tendency to duality; it can cause complications.

Your well-being

The Geminian body area covers the arms and hands, and these are therefore likely to be vulnerable. Make sure you find a hobby that encourages you to use your fingers

The Moon in Gemini

energetically; this should help avoid developing any Capricornian stiffness of the joints.

You will probably enjoy fast-moving and intellectually demanding exercise. Your low boredom threshold may, however, prove a problem when it comes to this area of your life, so endeavor to persevere.

Planning ahead
You could be less successful in organizing your financial affairs than many of your Capricornian brothers and sisters. Indeed, you may be among the few Capricornian Sun and Moon combinations who should seek financial advice when they have money to invest.

Parenthood
You keep up with your children's ideas and may sometimes even be ahead of them. Beware that you do not respond to your children too critically. Logic is admirable, but a hug and some real enthusiasm are also reassuring and encouraging.

THE MOON IN
CANCER

CAPRICORN AND CANCER ARE OPPOSITE OR POLAR ZODIAC SIGNS,
WHICH MEANS THAT YOU WERE BORN UNDER A FULL MOON.
YOU MAY BE RATHER PRONE TO RESTLESSNESS, BUT HAVE A WARM,
EMOTIONAL RESPONSE TO OTHER PEOPLE.

Each of us is, in one way or another, likely to express the attitudes of our polar, or opposite, Zodiac sign. Every sign has its partner across the horoscope; for you this is Cancer and, since the Moon was in that sign when you were born, the polarity is strongly emphasized. As the Moon also rules Cancer, its influence on you is extremely potent.

Self-expression
The influence of your Moon sign encourages you to respond warmly and sensitively to other people, but it may also mean that you have a defensive system that springs into action whenever you are challenged. It is possible that you are not particularly self-confident.

Romance
You are far more emotional than many Sun sign Capricornians and are prepared to give a great deal of yourself in a relationship. Being a very responsive lover, you will instinctively know how to please your partner sexually. You should be aware, however, that your desire to create a warm and secure environment could make it somewhat claustrophobic.

You are a natural worrier and this, plus a very powerful imagination, means that you can work yourself up into a positive frenzy if, for instance, your partner is simply late arriving home. You would be best advised to direct your imagination creatively.

Your well-being
The Cancerian body area covers the chest and breasts. There is no connection between the name of this sign and that of the disease but, as always, it is desirable for women to examine their breasts regularly.

The tendency to worry can affect your digestion, and your food could upset you when you are worried.

The Moon in Cancer

Restlessness could also affect your health. A relaxation technique like yoga may offset the tendency.

Planning ahead
As well as being a practical Capricornian, you have an instinctive shrewdness that comes from your Cancerian Moon. You are good at making your money work for you and should follow your instincts, especially when you are planning to make an investment.

You may sometimes feel that you are less well off than is the case. You will do well to review your financial situation from time to time, just to reassure yourself that you can, in fact, allow yourself to enjoy the fruits of your labors more wholeheartedly than you at first thought.

Parenthood
You make a wonderfully caring parent. You may, however, tend to resent it when your children decide to leave home; you should take up some new and demanding interest that will fill the gap. Make a conscious effort to keep up with your children's opinions and concerns, in order to avoid difficulties with the generation gap.

THE MOON IN
LEO

ALLOW THE WARMTH OF YOUR FIERY LEO MOON TO COLOR YOUR
PERSONALITY AND REACTIONS, AND TO INCREASE YOUR
ORGANIZATIONAL ABILITY. BE VERY CAREFUL, HOWEVER, THAT
YOU DO NOT LAPSE INTO POMPOSITY AND BOSSINESS.

The fire of your Moon sign adds warmth and an optimistic enthusiasm to your response to challenges. Your instinctive organizational ability readily springs into action and, in most situations, you probably end up well in control.

Self-expression
When taking matters into your own hands, as you almost invariably do, remember to smile and charm people, so that you can achieve your objectives without being accused of undue autocracy.

Most people with a Leo emphasis have creative potential. Music, acting, wood carving, or painting could all appeal to you.

Romance
Leo and Capricorn have a fine sense of style and are not averse to showing off. This quality will certainly be in the forefront when you fall in love.

Avoid bossiness at all times and, if you are accused of it, take the allegation seriously. It could detract from a relationship that would otherwise be good fun.

Your well-being
The Leo body area covers the spine and back, and you should exercise regularly to keep your spine supple. If you spend a great deal of time behind a desk, get a back-support chair.

The Leo organ is the heart, and it must be kept well exercised if it is to serve you long and well. You probably enjoy the usual Capricornian outdoor sports, like hiking and jogging, but may also be attracted to something that is a little more aesthetic, such as dancing or skating.

Planning ahead
Although in many ways Capricorn and Leo are very unlike each other, they have at least one thing in common:

The Moon in Leo

they both love and really appreciate true quality, and have somewhat expensive tastes.

There is a difference between them even here, however. Leos usually spend on quality simply because they get such a kick out of doing so, while Capricornians often spend money on impressing other people, particularly those who may be useful to them. One way or the other, you will undoubtedly end up spending a great deal of money. If your Sun sign makes you feel somewhat guilty about this, bear in mind that you generally invest wisely

and are sensible about saving. You will probably not need to get professional financial advice when you have money to invest.

Parenthood

You have what it takes to be a marvelous parent, as long as you do not allow a distance to yawn between you and your children. Follow your instinct and express warm enthusiasm; encourage your children when they show you the results of their latest efforts. If you keep up with their opinions and concerns, you will avoid the generation gap.

THE MOON IN
VIRGO

ALWAYS ALLOW THE AMBITIOUS, ASPIRING CAPRICORNIAN ELEMENTS
OF YOUR PERSONALITY FREE EXPRESSION, AND TRY NOT TO BE
HELD BACK BY INTUITIVE FEELINGS OF INFERIORITY. YOU MAY BE A
WORRIER, BUT YOU WILL ALSO BE A GOOD COMMUNICATOR.

Both Capricorn and Virgo are earth signs and, as a result, you are extremely practical, with an above-average amount of straightforward, basic common sense.

Self-expression
You approach problems in a rational, logical way, although you may become rather nervous and lack self-confidence when challenged or confronted with tricky situations. If this happens, try to develop a little more Capricornian coolness.

You have a sharp and analytical mind, and are marvelous at assessing problems in detail. In doing so, do not ignore the overall pattern. Develop breadth of vision; it will be of great advantage to you.

You may be rather shy, and to cover this tend to assume a chilly, aloof air. If you were strictly brought up, it may be that you were put down by your parents once or twice too often, and

that this has inhibited you a little more than it might have with other people. No doubt you have what it takes to rationalize such a background, and to deal with any problem that may have arisen as a result of it.

Romance
While you are a naturally adept communicator, you may not find it very easy to talk about your emotions. Do not be too modest. Try to relax and let your relationship develop.

Virgoans can be very critical, and you should beware of nagging your partners too much.

Your well-being
The Virgoan body area is the stomach. You really need a high-fiber diet, and could be attracted to vegetarianism. You are probably exceptionally susceptible to worry, and this will definitely affect your stomach.

The Moon in Virgo

Because you have a great deal of nervous energy, you may be prone to stress and tension, and could find it difficult to sit still, let alone really relax. A study of yoga or some other relaxation technique will go a long way toward conquering the problem.

Planning ahead

You are usually careful and very practical with money. You may, in fact, be somewhat too cautious and go for such safe investments that your money might not be working as hard for you as it could. Study various investment programs; your critical nature will ensure that you will benefit a great deal by doing so.

Parenthood

While you are fair in dealing with your children, you could respond to them more critically than you realize, which could damage their self-confidence. Encourage them; they may be just as ambitious as you are.

THE MOON IN
LIBRA

YOUR LIBRAN MOON MAKES YOU VERY DIPLOMATIC, AND YOU
HAVE THE ABILITY TO CHARM OTHERS. YOU RESPOND
WELL TO AN ENJOYABLE SOCIAL LIFE, BUT MAY SOMETIMES
SUCCUMB TO SNOBBISH SOCIAL CLIMBING.

Your Sun sign and your Moon sign are both cardinal signs, and as a result you are outgoing. You can develop excellent sympathy, even empathy, with other people.

Self-expression

When you are confronted by tricky situations, your initial response may be rather hesitant. Your Capricornian determination then takes over, letting you know where you stand and what you should do.

You live a full and busy life but, because you always find time for other people, especially if they are in trouble, you can give the impression that you are at best laid-back and, at worst, lazy. The latter is certainly not true, and neither, really, is the former.

Romance

You will probably not feel psychologically whole until you have contrived a satisfying and permanent partnership for yourself. You really do need that all-important rapport with another person who is close to you. But you also need space and time to yourself. When choosing a partner, it is important to keep this in mind.

You are among the more romantic of Sun sign Capricornians and will enjoy the most memorable, and often expensive and luxurious, occasions with your lovers.

Your well-being

The Libran body area is the kidneys, and if you suffer from constant headaches, it might be worth getting a checkup in case you have a slight kidney disorder. The lumbar region of the back is also Libra-ruled. If you suffer from pain in this region, get a back-support chair or follow a series of back-oriented exercises.

You could be less enthusiastic about exercise than most Sun sign Capricornians. Since you may also

The Moon in Libra

enjoy rich, sweet food, you could be vulnerable to weight gain. You need to exercise in a place where there is a pleasant social life – for example, in a friendly health club or gym.

Planning ahead

You are probably among the least careful of Capricornians where money is concerned. You may not waste it, but will like to own beautiful things.

Capricorn will rule at times when you have money to invest. If, however, you know that you tend not to save too determinedly, you would probably be wise to seek independent professional financial advice.

Parenthood

You will be a kind parent, as responsive to your children's needs as to everyone else's. Do not, however, let Libran indecision come between you and your children. Help them to aspire; your encouragement will pay off in the long run. Because you are always fair and attentive, you should leap across the generation gap.

THE MOON IN
SCORPIO

YOU POSSESS A POWERFUL SOURCE OF EMOTIONAL ENERGY THAT
INCREASES YOUR CAPRICORNIAN DETERMINATION TO
SUCCEED IN ALL OF YOUR OBJECTIVES. BEWARE, HOWEVER,
OF DEVELOPING OBSESSIVE TENDENCIES.

The earth element of your
Capricornian Sun and the water
element of your Scorpio Moon blend
well. You should be able to get the
best out of both of these influences.

Self-expression
You have intense emotional and
physical energy that springs into
action the moment you are
challenged. Combined with
Capricornian determination and
ambition, this gives you the potential
to be extremely successful.

It is important for you to be
emotionally involved in your work. If
you are merely working at some
boring job in order to make money,
your motivation and energies will
stagnate. Try some self-analysis if you
feel any danger signals, and make
changes if necessary.

Be careful not to be too ruthless
with your colleagues. You would be
wise to remember the old saying: do

not tread on people on the way up,
since you may well encounter them
again on the way down.

Romance
Your powerful emotions make you a
passionate lover who needs a rich and
fulfilling love and sex life. You will be
a demanding partner and will need an
enthusiastic lover.

The worst Scorpio fault is jealousy,
and it might be that you occasionally
succumb to this useless, negative
emotion. Listen to rational
explanations from your partner.

Your well-being
The Scorpio body area covers the
genitals. Men with this Sun and Moon
combination should regularly examine
their testicles for irregularities, and
women should have cervical smears.

Scorpios usually enjoy living it up,
which means eating rich food and
drinking fine wine. As a result, you

The Moon in Scorpio

may have a tendency to put on excess
weight. If you have to diet, you will
probably not find it easy; on reaching
your ideal weight, you may rush off
for a celebratory banquet. You may
enjoy the discipline and steady
routine of a regular sports interest.

Planning ahead

You should cope well with money and
may have a considerable flair for
making it. Your Sun and Moon sign
combination suggests that you are

good in business, and that you could
build a successful business of your
own. You should have no problems
when you have money to invest.

Parenthood

You have the capacity to enjoy
parenthood, but could be so involved
with your career that you may have
less time for your children than is
wise. Listen to your children, and
always encourage them in their
ambitions and interests.

THE MOON IN
SAGITTARIUS

SAGITTARIAN BREADTH OF VISION AND ABILITY TO ACCEPT
CHALLENGE WORKS WELL WITH YOUR STRONG CAPRICORNIAN
AMBITION. YOUR CAPRICORNIAN SENSE OF
HUMOR IS FUELED BY YOUR SAGITTARIAN MOON.

The influence of your Sagittarian Moon adds some remarkably varied qualities to your personality. By expressing them you should be able to achieve a great deal.

Self-expression
Your Moon sign gives you a natural optimism, but there could be conflict here, for Sun sign Capricornians can sometimes be pessimistic and gloomy. If you tend to swing between one mood and another, try to allow Capricornian common sense and ambition to override gloom and doom.

You have a good mind and a good intellect. Do not let them stagnate; it is important for you to have an intellectual challenge of some kind, perhaps a language.

Romance
Sagittarius is a warm, loving, and emotional sign. You will not find it difficult to express these qualities.

You are passionate and will want to enjoy a rich and rewarding love and sex life. Perhaps you do not take this sphere of your life as seriously as do others of your Sun sign, but the chances are that you get a lot more fun out of it. You need a measure of freedom within a relationship and should bear this in mind when considering a permanent liaison.

The worst Sagittarian fault is restlessness. Try not to take this out on your partner, or to allow that ever-so-slightly roving eye to cause too many problems.

Your well-being
The Sagittarian body area covers the hips and thighs, and women with this sign emphasized are prone to putting on weight around this area. Special exercises will help and should encourage good muscle tone. A diet of lighter food than you may like is also advisable.

The Moon in Sagittarius

The Sagittarian organ is the liver and, because it is common for people of that sign to enjoy rich, meaty foods, heavy desserts, wine, and beer, it might be wise to keep some hangover cures handy. Keep generally active with energy-consuming interests and you will thrive.

Planning ahead

Although you are practical to a fault and sensible with money, you may have a deeply ingrained gambling instinct. You are likely to enjoy the occasional financial risk, and this may take the form of a bet on a big race or some marginally unsavory stock purchase. For the most part, you can easily control this tendency. When making important financial decisions, seek the advice of an expert.

Parenthood

You will be a lively and enthusiastic parent, eager to stimulate your children's minds and to encourage their efforts. Be ambitious for them without being too heavy-handed. You should have few problems with the generation gap and will find coping with older children somewhat easier than understanding toddlers.

THE MOON IN
CAPRICORN

BECAUSE BOTH THE SUN AND THE MOON WERE IN CAPRICORN AT
THE TIME OF YOUR BIRTH, YOU WERE BORN UNDER A
NEW MOON. THEREFORE THE EARTH ELEMENT POWERFULLY
EMPHASIZES YOUR PERSONALITY AND REACTIONS.

When you read a list of the characteristics of your practical, aspiring Sun sign, you will probably recognize that a great many of them apply to you. On average, out of a list of perhaps 20 personality traits of a Sun sign, most people will identify with 11 or 12. For you, the average increases considerably, as both the Sun and the Moon were in Capricorn when you were born.

Self-expression
The influence of your Moon sign encourages you to appreciate ambitious schemes and daunting projects, which you will usually want to accept as soon as they are put to you. You may, however, tend to swing between positive, ambitious thinking and a negative, self-doubting attitude.

No doubt you have the marvelous, offbeat sense of humor that is so characteristic of Capricorn, and it will surface very spontaneously. But you are not beyond slumping into a grumbling mood and complaining that nothing is right with your world. Try to allow the positive side of your personality to dominate.

Romance
You may not express your emotions very freely. This is probably due to your natural Capricornian caution and your self-protective instinct.

Once committed, you are very faithful and will enjoy a rich, rewarding love and sex life. You will be ambitious for your partner's progress in life, but it is possible that you may have slightly old-fashioned or conventional ideas as to how your relationship should develop.

Your well-being
The pages dedicated to health and well-being (*pages 22 to 23*) are especially relevant to you, as your vulnerabilities are extremely

The Moon in Capricorn

Capricornian. You could be even more prone to rheumatic pain and arthritis than most Sun sign Capricornians.

Planning ahead

You will not be averse to making an effort to impress important people. On the whole, however, you will use your money well, although you may sometimes think you are less well off than you actually are. Make an effort to follow your naturally cautious instinct when investing, and you will not go far wrong.

Parenthood

You will want to do a lot for your children and will work hard to this end. However, because you are always busy, you may not spend as much time with them as you should, and they may feel that you are a rather distant parent.

You will be conventional in your attitude and could be rather strict. This is all right, provided that you make an effort to understand your children's concerns and problems, and thus avoid the generation gap.

THE MOON IN
AQUARIUS

YOU MAY NEED TO BE INDEPENDENT, BUT TRY TO AVOID GAINING
A REPUTATION FOR BEING COOL AND DISTANT. WHILE YOU ARE
ATTRACTED TO THE UNCONVENTIONAL, YOU WILL ALWAYS WANT
TO DO WHAT IS CONSIDERED ACCEPTABLE.

Aquarius and Capricorn are neighboring Zodiac signs and, until the discovery of Uranus in the eighteenth century, the planet Saturn ruled them both. They therefore have a certain amount in common, but in some respects they could not be more different. Your Capricornian Sun, for instance, inclines you toward conventionality in outlook and manner, while your Aquarian Moon sometimes makes you respond to situations in an unconventional way.

Self-expression

Both Capricorn and Aquarius share the tendency not to show emotion very freely. While you have a dynamic, magnetic personality that is very attractive to the opposite sex, you may instinctively send out vibes telling admirers that, while they may certainly admire you, they should also keep their distance. In spite of this, you have a romantic streak that is

quite wonderful once ignited. Another aspect of your attitude to romance is that you may put off deepening an emotional relationship, or certainly committing yourself to marriage, for longer than most people. This is probably because you enjoy your independence so much.

Your well-being

The Aquarian body area covers the ankles, which are vulnerable. You may well enjoy wearing fashion shoes and could easily twist your ankle. The circulation is also Aquarius-ruled, and yours may not be too brisk, so make sure you wear several layers of light clothes in cold weather.

You will like various forms of exercise, particularly if they are an outlet for your creative flair; all kinds of dance, or perhaps skating, will probably suit you. Exercise will aid your circulation and is excellent for preventing Capricornian stiffness and

The Moon in Aquarius

rheumatic pain. Aim to keep your diet on the light side. Many Capricornians favor the great classical dishes of the world; you probably do best on poultry, fish, and a salads.

Planning ahead

You will spend money more freely than most Capricornians and may well be attracted to exciting, but perhaps not very sound, investment schemes. You must aim to be careful and should not gamble any more than you can afford to lose. In all situations, allow your Capricornian common sense to rule the day.

Parenthood

You will make a lively and well-informed parent. You should not find the generation gap to be a problem, provided that the strict, conventional Capricornian side of your personality balances your unconventional Moon sign. Bear in mind that children like to know where they stand.

THE MOON IN
PISCES

YOUR PISCEAN MOON HEIGHTENS YOUR EMOTIONAL LEVEL, AND
WARMS AND SENSITIZES YOUR REACTIONS. YOU
MAY, HOWEVER, NEED TO CONSCIOUSLY BUILD SELF-CONFIDENCE.
DO NOT SMOTHER YOUR CAPRICORNIAN AMBITION.

Your earth sign Sun and water sign Moon combine well. As a Capricornian, you are practical and cautious, but you will respond sensitively to situations and should not find it difficult to show tender emotion. You may not, however, be very self-confident and could have to make a conscious effort to allow your positive, aspiring, and ambitious Capricornian qualities full expression.

Self-expression
Because you are sensitive, there is a chance that you may have suffered more deeply than most people from parental put-downs. This could have made you fearful of taking firm steps onward and upward. Make an effort to develop your ambitions and to summon up the inner strength to achieve them.

You are a warm, kind person, who could do especially well in a career in the caring professions.

Romance
You respond warmly and lovingly to partners and are capable of a truly rewarding love and sex life. The worst Piscean fault is deceptiveness. As a Capricornian you will loathe this characteristic and should therefore be able to combat it successfully.

When you fall in love, you may have a tendency to see your partner through rose-colored glasses. Consciously allow your Capricornian qualities full expression, especially when considering a long-term commitment. Never slip into the bad habit of telling white lies in order not to hurt your partner since, in the long run, the implications could be ghastly.

Your well-being
The Piscean body area covers the feet, and yours are vulnerable. You may well enjoy going barefoot, but be careful: you are more vulnerable than most people to foot infections.

The Moon in Pisces

Pisceans tend to put on weight rather easily, usually because of a reliance on junk food. Capricornians are often lean, or perhaps even gaunt. If you do have a slow metabolism, you will need to keep a careful check on your diet. Exercise such as dancing, swimming, and downhill or cross-country skiing will help a lot.

Planning ahead

Pisceans are generally not too good at handling money, and your immediate reaction to financial problems may well be one of utter confusion. Do not make sudden decisions if you have money to invest, and be careful not to fall for get-rich-quick schemes. Let your Capricornian gift for finance overrule any Piscean impracticality.

Parenthood

You will be a good parent, who will sensitively and intuitively understand your children's needs. If you follow your Piscean instincts when dealing with your children, they will always work well, and you will have very few problems with the generation gap. Always remember to express warmth and tenderness to children, as well as Capricornian forthrightness.

CAPRICORN
MOON CHARTS

THE FOLLOWING TABLES WILL ENABLE YOU TO DISCOVER YOUR
MOON SIGN. THEN, BY REFERRING TO THE PRECEDING
PAGES, YOU WILL BE ABLE TO INVESTIGATE ITS QUALITIES, AND
SEE HOW THEY WORK WITH YOUR SUN SIGN.

By referring to the charts on pages 57, 58 and 59 locate the Zodiacal glyph for the month of the year in which you were born. Using the Moon table on this page, find the number opposite the day you were born that month. Then, starting from the glyph you found first, count off that number using the list of Zodiacal glyphs (below, right). You may have to count to Pisces and continue with Aries. For example, if you were born on May 21, 1991, first you need to find the Moon sign on the chart on page 59. Look down the chart to May; the glyph is Sagittarius (♐). Then consult the Moon table for the 21st. It tells you to add nine glyphs. Starting from Sagittarius, count down nine, and you find your Moon sign is Virgo (♍).

MOON TABLE

DAYS OF THE MONTH AND NUMBER OF
SIGNS THAT SHOULD BE ADDED

DAY	ADD	DAY	ADD	DAY	ADD	DAY	ADD
1	0	9	4	17	7	25	11
2	1	10	4	18	8	26	11
3	1	11	5	19	8	27	12
4	1	12	5	20	9	28	12
5	2	13	5	21	9	29	1
6	2	14	6	22	10	30	1
7	3	15	6	23	10	31	2
8	3	16	7	24	10		

ZODIACAL GLYPHS

♈	Aries
♉	Taurus
♊	Gemini
♋	Cancer
♌	Leo
♍	Virgo
♎	Libra
♏	Scorpio
♐	Sagittarius
♑	Capricorn
♒	Aquarius
♓	Pisces

	1923	1924	1925	1926	1927	1928	1929	1930	1931	1932	1933	1934	1935
JAN	♊	♏	♈	♌	♐	♈	♍	♑	♉	♎	♓	♋	♏
FEB	♌	♐	♉	♍	♑	♊	♏	♓	♋	♐	♈	♌	♑
MAR	♌	♑	♉	♍	♒	♋	♍	♓	♋	♐	♉	♍	♑
APR	♎	♓	♋	♏	♈	♍	♑	♉	♍	♒	♊	♎	♓
MAY	♏	♈	♌	♐	♉	♎	♒	♊	♎	♓	♋	♐	♈
JUN	♑	♉	♍	♒	♋	♏	♓	♌	♐	♉	♍	♑	♊
JUL	♒	♋	♏	♓	♌	♐	♈	♍	♑	♊	♎	♓	♋
AUG	♈	♌	♐	♉	♍	♒	♊	♏	♓	♋	♐	♈	♌
SEP	♉	♎	♒	♋	♏	♓	♌	♐	♈	♍	♑	♊	♎
OCT	♊	♏	♓	♌	♐	♉	♍	♑	♉	♎	♓	♋	♏
NOV	♌	♑	♉	♍	♑	♊	♏	♓	♋	♐	♈	♌	♑
DEC	♍	♒	♊	♎	♓	♌	♐	♈	♌	♑	♉	♍	♒

	1936	1937	1938	1939	1940	1941	1942	1943	1944	1945	1946	1947	1948
JAN	♈	♌	♑	♉	♍	♒	♊	♎	♓	♌	♐	♈	♍
FEB	♉	♎	♒	♊	♏	♈	♌	♐	♉	♍	♑	♊	♎
MAR	♊	♎	♒	♍	♐	♈	♌	♐	♉	♎	♒	♊	♏
APR	♌	♐	♈	♈	♑	♉	♎	♒	♋	♏	♓	♌	♑
MAY	♍	♑	♉	♎	♒	♊	♏	♓	♌	♐	♉	♍	♒
JUN	♎	♒	♋	♏	♈	♌	♑	♉	♎	♒	♊	♏	♓
JUL	♏	♈	♌	♑	♉	♍	♒	♊	♏	♓	♌	♐	♈
AUG	♑	♉	♎	♒	♋	♏	♈	♌	♐	♉	♍	♑	♊
SEP	♓	♋	♏	♈	♌	♑	♉	♍	♒	♋	♏	♓	♌
OCT	♈	♌	♑	♉	♎	♒	♊	♎	♓	♌	♐	♈	♍
NOV	♊	♎	♒	♊	♏	♈	♌	♐	♉	♍	♑	♊	♏
DEC	♋	♏	♓	♌	♑	♉	♍	♑	♊	♎	♒	♋	♐

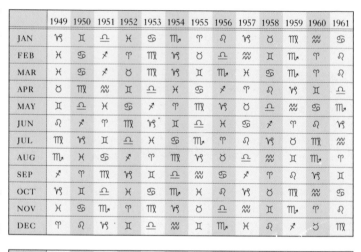

	1949	1950	1951	1952	1953	1954	1955	1956	1957	1958	1959	1960	1961
JAN	♑	♊	♎	♓	♋	♏	♈	♌	♑	♉	♍	♒	♋
FEB	♓	♋	♐	♈	♍	♑	♉	♎	♒	♊	♏	♈	♌
MAR	♓	♋	♐	♉	♍	♑	♊	♏	♓	♋	♏	♈	♌
APR	♉	♍	♒	♊	♎	♓	♋	♐	♈	♌	♑	♊	♎
MAY	♊	♎	♓	♋	♐	♈	♍	♑	♉	♎	♒	♋	♏
JUN	♌	♐	♈	♍	♑	♊	♎	♓	♋	♐	♈	♌	♑
JUL	♍	♑	♊	♎	♓	♋	♏	♈	♌	♑	♉	♍	♒
AUG	♏	♓	♋	♐	♈	♍	♑	♉	♎	♒	♊	♏	♈
SEP	♐	♈	♍	♑	♊	♎	♒	♋	♐	♈	♌	♑	♊
OCT	♑	♊	♎	♓	♋	♏	♓	♌	♑	♉	♍	♒	♋
NOV	♓	♋	♏	♈	♍	♑	♉	♎	♒	♊	♍	♈	♌
DEC	♈	♌	♑	♊	♎	♒	♊	♏	♓	♌	♐	♉	♍

	1962	1963	1964	1965	1966	1967	1968	1969	1970	1971	1972	1973	1974
JAN	♏	♓	♌	♐	♈	♍	♑	♊	♎	♒	♋	♐	♈
FEB	♐	♉	♍	♒	♊	♏	♓	♋	♏	♈	♍	♑	♉
MAR	♐	♉	♎	♒	♊	♏	♈	♌	♐	♉	♍	♑	♊
APR	♒	♋	♏	♈	♌	♑	♉	♍	♒	♊	♏	♓	♋
MAY	♓	♌	♐	♉	♍	♒	♊	♎	♓	♋	♐	♈	♍
JUN	♉	♎	♒	♊	♏	♓	♌	♐	♉	♍	♑	♊	♎
JUL	♊	♏	♓	♌	♐	♈	♍	♑	♊	♎	♓	♋	♐
AUG	♌	♐	♉	♎	♒	♊	♏	♓	♋	♏	♈	♍	♑
SEP	♍	♒	♋	♏	♓	♋	♐	♉	♍	♑	♊	♎	♓
OCT	♏	♓	♌	♐	♈	♍	♒	♊	♎	♒	♋	♐	♈
NOV	♐	♉	♎	♒	♊	♎	♓	♋	♐	♈	♍	♑	♉
DEC	♑	♊	♏	♓	♋	♐	♈	♌	♑	♉	♎	♒	♊

	1975	1976	1977	1978	1979	1980	1981	1982	1983	1984	1985	1986	1987
JAN	♌	♑	♉	♍	♒	♊	♏	♓	♌	♐	♉	♍	♑
FEB	♎	♒	♋	♏	♈	♌	♐	♉	♍	♒	♊	♎	♓
MAR	♎	♓	♋	♏	♈	♍	♑	♉	♎	♒	♊	♏	♓
APR	♐	♈	♍	♑	♊	♎	♒	♋	♏	♈	♌	♑	♉
MAY	♑	♉	♎	♒	♋	♏	♓	♌	♐	♉	♍	♒	♊
JUN	♓	♋	♐	♈	♌	♑	♉	♎	♒	♊	♏	♓	♌
JUL	♈	♌	♑	♉	♍	♒	♋	♏	♓	♌	♐	♉	♍
AUG	♉	♎	♓	♋	♏	♈	♌	♐	♈	♎	♒	♊	♎
SEP	♋	♐	♈	♌	♐	♊	♎	♒	♊	♏	♓	♌	♐
OCT	♌	♑	♉	♍	♒	♋	♏	♓	♋	♐	♉	♍	♑
NOV	♎	♓	♋	♏	♓	♌	♐	♉	♍	♒	♊	♎	♓
DEC	♏	♈	♌	♐	♉	♍	♑	♊	♎	♓	♋	♐	♈

	1988	1989	1990	1991	1992	1993	1994	1995	1996	1997	1998	1999	2000
JAN	♊	♎	♒	♋	♏	♈	♌	♑	♉	♎	♒	♊	♏
FEB	♋	♐	♈	♍	♑	♉	♎	♒	♋	♏	♈	♌	♐
MAR	♌	♐	♉	♍	♒	♊	♎	♓	♋	♏	♈	♌	♑
APR	♍	♒	♊	♏	♓	♋	♐	♈	♍	♑	♊	♎	♓
MAY	♏	♓	♌	♐	♈	♍	♑	♉	♎	♒	♋	♏	♈
JUN	♐	♉	♍	♑	♊	♎	♓	♋	♐	♈	♌	♑	♉
JUL	♑	♊	♎	♒	♋	♐	♈	♌	♑	♉	♎	♒	♋
AUG	♓	♌	♐	♈	♍	♑	♉	♎	♓	♋	♏	♓	♌
SEP	♉	♍	♑	♊	♏	♓	♋	♏	♈	♌	♑	♉	♎
OCT	♊	♎	♒	♋	♐	♈	♌	♑	♉	♎	♒	♊	♏
NOV	♌	♐	♈	♍	♑	♉	♎	♒	♋	♏	♈	♌	♑
DEC	♍	♑	♉	♎	♒	♋	♏	♈	♌	♐	♉	♍	♒

THE SOLAR SYSTEM

THE STARS, OTHER THAN THE SUN, PLAY NO PART IN THE SCIENCE
OF ASTROLOGY. ASTROLOGERS USE ONLY THE BODIES IN THE
SOLAR SYSTEM, EXCLUDING THE EARTH, TO CALCULATE HOW OUR
LIVES AND PERSONALITIES CHANGE.

Pluto
Pluto takes 246 years to travel around
the Sun. It affects our unconscious
instincts and urges, gives us strength
in difficulty, and perhaps emphasizes
any inherent cruel streak.

Neptune
Neptune stays in each sign for 14
years. At best it makes us sensitive
and imaginative; at worst it
encourages deceit and carelessness,
making us worry.

Uranus
The influence of Uranus can make us
friendly, kind, eccentric, inventive,
and unpredictable.

Saturn
In ancient times, Saturn was the most
distant known planet. Its influence
can limit our ambition and make us
either overly cautious (but practical),
or reliable and self-disciplined.

SATURN

PLUTO

NEPTUNE

URANUS

Jupiter

Jupiter encourages expansion, optimism, generosity, and breadth of vision. It can, however, also make us wasteful, extravagant, and conceited.

Mars

Much associated with energy, anger, violence, selfishness, and a strong sex drive, Mars also encourages decisiveness and leadership.

JUPITER

Earth

Every planet contributes to the environment of the Solar System, and a person born on Venus would no doubt be influenced by our own planet in some way.

The Moon

Although it is a satellite of the Earth, the Moon is known in astrology as a planet. It lies about 240,000 miles from the Earth and, astrologically, is second in importance to the Sun.

MERCURY

THE MOON

VENUS

MARS

EARTH

The Sun

The Sun, the only star used by astrologers, influences the way we present ourselves to the world – our image or personality; the face we show to other people.

Venus

The planet of love and partnership, Venus can emphasize all our best personal qualities. It may also encourage us to be lazy, impractical, and too dependent on other people.

Mercury

The planet closest to the Sun affects our intellect. It can make us inquisitive, versatile, argumentative, perceptive, and clever, but maybe also inconsistent, cynical, and sarcastic.